# 4 Steps to Affiliate Marketing Success

## Simple Tips for Your Passive Income

### By Joseph Davidson

# CONTENTS

## Step 3 – Be familiar with your audience

What is an audience?

Why it is so important to know your audience?

Who is your audience?


## Step 4 – Use all productive methods of promoting

Websites

Getting a domain name

Using a hosting service

Establishing a website

Writing content

SEO (search engine optimization)

Blogs

# Introduction

Often most people come across many difficulties on their ways of affiliate business, feel themselves weak for overcoming barriers, meet unknown issues there, feel disappointed and finally give up everything. That's miserable! Because, they have just missed something to do right and for this reason they are going to the wrong way.

When I have heard about affiliate marketing initially it seemed to me as a hard to do and unreachable task. The lack of knowledge about affiliate business made me fear about failures and blinded my eyes for seeing amazing successes that many super affiliates are reaching today.

After a short time I decided to change my mind and attitude to affiliate marketing. Then I started to study affiliate marketing deeper and wider. Researched a lot, tried to learn other affiliate's ways and methods as much as possible and made my own conclusions. Days, weeks and months passed. At the end all gathered materials: tips, recommendations, strategies, tricks, dos and don'ts and others turned into a useful guide which you are going to read now.

The guide which was created personally helped me to discover the right path in this business. Several months ago without this guide I was staying on this dilemma:

- *How can I do it..?*
- *Is it possible to reach actual results..?*
- *May I begin it without any capital..?*
- *What happens, if..?*

But today all doubts and uncertain feelings are blown away from my mind.

**So what kind of book this is?**

This book can be a practical guide for affiliates, especially for beginners. This helps them to increase their knowledge, correct their mistakes and direct them into the right path of affiliate marketing.

By writing my current book, I have tried to reveal some affiliate marketing secrets, shared my knowledge and experiences and of course tried to be frank you.

**Dear reader! Remember, this is not:**

- A comprehensive book of affiliate marketing;
- A personal success story;
- A flashing "Trust me and make millions!" deception;
- A "Buy my proven money making system", etc.

While reading this book you may get knowledge about how to select the right niche, how to establish an audience and platform, how to use free and paid promoting methods and many others.

While writing this book I have tried to be short, concrete and honest, instead of spinning your mind with flashing, dishonest and empty promises. I hope you'll understand me at the end of the reading.

Besides, at the end of each chapter I've provided you with some top and useful websites related to the subject. I believe that these recommended websites will be helpful and makes your hard work easier.

If my current book helps you to reach some valuable achievements in your affiliate business I will feel myself really happy.

# Step 1 – About affiliate marketing

## What is affiliate marketing?

Affiliate marketing is one of the types of Internet businesses and a form of performance based marketing in which affiliates get commissions for their promoting endeavors.

There are four major participants in affiliate marketing: the merchant, the network, the affiliate and the customer.

As a merchant it may be any brand or person, a network gives offers for affiliates and takes care of the payments, an affiliate promotes affiliate products or services for a commission and a customer purchases the stuff promoted by affiliates.

Usually affiliates insert hosting links, banners or product reviews on their blogs, websites, social networks, viral products, etc. When visitors click on these affiliate links and make a purchase, affiliates will get a commission from this sale.

For this affiliates need to be a member of any affiliate program or system. After being a member and getting their account, they will choose and then promote products or services by using various easy and even more complicated methods.

## Benefits of affiliate marketing

Here are some advantages of being an affiliate marketer:

- *Zero or little business investment.* In affiliate marketing you can start with little or without any financial investment. Most successful affiliates invest some little money for establishing their websites and blogs. But some of them even start without any money using just free promoting methods like forums, revenue sharing websites, viral products, social media, etc.

- *Time and money freedom.* For succeeding in affiliate business you don't need to any employees or special working hours. Everything depends on you. The more time and effort you deposit, the more money and success you get.  Because in affiliate marketing income is not limited and it is almost up to you how much to work and how much to earn. For example, once successfully created affiliate business or good written product review may turn into a passive income, which may bring capital even when you are not working.

- **High diversity.** Affiliate marketing can fit almost any person and any subject you're interested in. There are various profitable subjects (niches) that you can find, promote and make nice incomes from them.

- **Without expert knowledge.** It isn't necessary to be an expert in the field you are working and promoting affiliate stuffs. For example, if you are promoting skin care products, you don't need to be a dermatologist or a skin care specialist. All you have to do is advertising and marketing these affiliate products properly and professionally.

- **Limitless programs.** There are many affiliate programs and networks on the Internet which you may join and make excellent profits from them.

**Recommended affiliate networks for joining:**

- www.amazon.com
- www.e-bay.com
- www.clickbank.com
- www.cj.com
- www.linkshare.com
- www.paydotcom.com

# Step 2 – Select the right niche

## What is a niche?

Word "niche" is one of the commonly used terms in affiliate marketing. It is a category or sub category that you choose in marketplace. Usually these categories may be different in every affiliate system and also are distinguished by their particularities.

Here is an example of a niche and its sub niches:

| | | |
|---|---|---|
| Bodybuilding | Exercises | Weight loss exercises |
| Arts | Music | New age music |
| Health and Beauty | Skin care | Acne |

# Why it's so important to choose the right niche?

Experts and top earning affiliates affirm that the essence of selecting the right niche is so high that it's almost impossible to get substantial results without choosing the right niche.

Here are two very considerable factors of choosing the niche:

- *It helps people quicker find what they search for.* Most internet users seek for something special and interesting for them. Only a small amount of people enter Internet without any clear purpose. For example, minorities of Internet users type in search engines as "food", but majorities of them write as "healthy food recipes", "weigh loss recipes", "recipes for beautiful skin", etc. This means if your site is not relevant to what people search for they will exit and go to somewhere else that is necessary for them.

- *It increases your search engine ranking.* If your web site is too general then the chances of getting high traffic will be so low. Search engines can't send you traffic if they don't know what your website is really about. Because they don't know whom to send you. Imagine your web site is about "Health and Beauty" and people are seeking for "Melanoma". In this case can you guarantee them to find the exact answer that they are seeking for? Will search engines send these people who are interested in this type of skin cancer to the website which is just about health and beauty? "No", of course. In this situation websites which are related to skin cancer problems will be more helpful.

Except these reasons selecting the right niche helps you to avoid from various traumatic situations and serves to prevent upcoming failures on your way of affiliate business.

## Which is the proper niche for you?

For defining the right niche you must know the exact answers for these three questions:

- *What are your interests or what you love to do?* It is clear to everybody that living and working with interests makes people happier and their life easier. One of the benefits of doing what you love is that you may not often feel many tedious difficulties which occur on your way and you may take pleasure by doing it. Therefore, choose a subject that you are really passionate about it.

- **_Are you good at the subject you have opted?_** You should always be aware of what you are promoting. Most successful affiliates appreciate that it is impossible and prosperity is not guaranteed if you are trying to move your affiliate business with not knowing the products you are promoting. How would you recommend something to people if you don't know it? I think it's dishonest and impossible. If possible, it will be short life opportunity. So, recommend and promote products or services which you have also tested them before.

- **_Do people spend money in the subject you have chosen?_** There are limitless high demand products and services on the Internet which people are seeking every day. But on the other hand these products and services will also be high competing and hard to win among other high skilled and experienced affiliates. But even so, it is also possible for you to endeavor and attain some substantial results almost in every market.

When you choose a subject for beginning don't just dive into the categories in the market. Do some research, don't go too broad and narrow your selection. For example, choose "Health and Fitness" category, narrow it to subject "Beauty" and then you may narrow it again to "10 tips for dry skin care", etc. This is really productive and helps you to avoid from high competition.

If you seek for a best selling product in a high demand, follow these useful tips:

- *Think about what people really seek and need for*. People on the Internet always search for something special. It may be an answer for their request, a solution for their problem or just appealing information.

- *Think about which products or services actually help and solve their problems.* If you promote helpless products or services, even if you use the greatest methods and techniques, people will not buy them. And the worst of all, later you may lose your all gathered reputation and credibility.

- **Think about what makes them completely satisfied and happy.** The only thing that makes customers pleased and happy is high quality and helpful products. They'll be delighted only when they get expected positive results after their purchase.

## Mistakes you should avoid

If you choose a wrong niche, your business will not grow and very soon you will meet with setbacks and adversities which can knock you out of the way. Therefore, it is vital for you to avoid these common mistakes when choosing a niche:

- **Not selecting a niche.** If you try to choose affiliate stuffs without opting your own niche and promote "everything under the Sun", believe me, sooner or later affiliate marketing will be fully disappointed and unsuccessful for you.
- **Grasping too much.** If you are trying to choose as many niches as you see and promote "everything under the Sun" or attempting to do everything in everywhere, believe me stressful and unsuccessful

days are coming to you. As I said before affiliate marketing is not about promoting everything to everybody when you meet them on your way.

- **Choosing low quality products.** Do you want to buy low quality product for yourself? The answer is "No". Of course, you want to be completely satisfied with the product you have acquired. So do others. Usually people will be more skeptical, cautious and eager to quit when they are going to pay money for something unknown. You may guess results and experience feelings when an unknown person is proposing you a low quality product.

- **Choosing too competitive products.** If there is high demand for a product, there will be also high competition. This may be difficult for you to succeed among other high skilled and qualified affiliates. If you are new in affiliate business, it's better to be little bit modest and get some knowledge and experience first. Don't rush! It takes time and effort to be successful in affiliate business.

- ***Choosing a product that you don't know.*** It's hard and sometimes impossible to promote products that you are not familiar with. Being aware of and then recommending it to someone is usually easier to sell. So, don't attempt to promote products which you haven't verified and unknown for you.

**Recommended websites:**

www.nichebot.com

# Step 3 – Be familiar with your audience

## What is an audience?

Audience is a visitor, reader or listener in your platform. As an audience there may be any kind of person. For example, an athlete, a student, a gardener, a physicist, an entrepneur, etc.

In audience interests and intentions may be various and special for each of them coming from their needs. For example, an athlete may be eager to develop his/her athletic skills; a student would like to obtain any foreign language study guide; a hair stylist tries to be aware of the latest hair styling techniques, etc.

## Why it is so important to know your audience?

Being familiar with your audience makes your job easier and serves to get faster affiliate successes. It helps you to provide your audience with what they actually need and this mean more purchases, more commissions and more achievements in your affiliate business.

## Who is your audience?

Determining your audience demands some research and little efforts from you. Answer to these questions to discover your audience:

- Who are your readers, listeners or visitors in your platform?
- What do they like and dislike?
- What does motivate them?
- What kind of products and characters do they like?
- Which keywords do they use?
- Why are they coming to you or what is attracting them?

**Recommended websites:**

- www.quantacast.com
- www.google.com/adplanner

# Step 4 – Use all productive methods of promoting

After choosing your affiliate product or service, you will necessarily need to promote them with any method. Though there are several ways and methods of promoting affiliate products or services on the Internet, sometimes many people can't use them productively and even don't be familiar with all of them.

Naturally, on the Internet exists high range of promoting ways and techniques, but each of them differs by its peculiarities, advantages and disadvantages.

Here we learn some of them.

## Websites

Without any doubt, applying your personal website as a primary promoting method is the biggest, most effective and easiest way of succeeding in affiliate business.

In your website you can centralize, gather all your created ads and proceedings, link other promoting methods with each other, etc. This is definitely easy manageable and comfortable for controlling your affiliate business.

There are two options for getting a website: *Buying a ready one* and *Building it personally*. Both of them have advantages and disadvantages.

If you absolutely don't know how to create a website and intend to buy a ready one, search for it on the Internet. There are numerous profitable and ready offers by website creators and owners.

But, most affiliates prefer creating their own website rather than just buying a ready one. But website creating and development takes not only more time and effort, but also requires some knowledge, skills and patience.

Usually winning and expedient website should be:

- Simple;
- Well designed;
- Well arranged;
- Easy to review;
- Informative;
- Inspiring;

- Helpful, etc.

When most people enter the Internet and then a website they often search for a solution for their problems. While searching on the Internet they feel these psychological feelings:

- *Need.* The majority of Internet users don't just enter websites; instead they get obvious goals and want something valuable.

- *Pain.* Every person in the world feels this physical and psychological feeling. Living without it is absolutely impossible and unavoidable. It doesn't matter what you offer them and how great your proposal seems; believe me, if you find a solution to their problems and suffers, they will also give you real value as a replacement for it.

- *Fear*. As fear it may be their awe of spending or losing money on a product they are going to buy, fear of getting negative results by using it, etc. In this case you have to provide them with trust, veracity and other helpful comprehensions to break their fear and anxiety.

- **Skeptics.** As some experts say only about two or three visitors out of hundred (or hundreds) may buy the stuff you are offering in your website. Others would be too skeptical and often leave your website with just a click of their mouse. So, if you wish hundreds of people buy your product, you have to make thousands or millions of them enter your web page.

**So, what you need to create a website?**

Website building is not a rocket science, but as I said before it takes time, little capital and endurance to be successful. For beginning you should know about how to get a domain name, web hosting, theme creating, mailing services, SEO (Search Engine Optimization), content writing, using necessary keywords, organizing website layout and many others.

Let's start learning them!

# Getting a domain name

Picking a good domain name is an essential part of web site creating. As your online identity it says a lot about you or your running industry.

Domain name is a part of a network address that identifies it as belonging to a particular field. For example: nytimes.com, harvard.edu, wikipedia.org, spain.info, sourceforge.net, etc.

Here are some tips for creating a successful domain name:

- *Select a name relevant to the field you choose.* The domain name of your website should reveal its main function and provide your readers with the first impression. When people see your domain name for the first time, they should promptly imagine what kind of content they may find in your web site. For example, when we see www.bodybuilding.com we instantly recognize this website is about bodybuilding. Besides this if you have a brand name you should give it or just use your primary keyword as a domain name.

- *Keep it short and simple.* Usually short names are easy to type and easy to remember. Simplicity and brevity is enough in this case.

- *Make it easy to remember*. If you select difficult and hard to keep in mind domain names, it may be complicated for site reviewers to recall it. That's why just give simple and easy to remember names for your domain.

- *Choose a catchy name.* Almost in every business choosing an attractive name plays a significant role for winning in this matter. Don't be unconcerned to this reality.

- *Don't use numbers and hyphens.* They may be confusing, hard for typing and not easy to remember.

- *Use popular domain extensions.* .COM, .ORG, .NET, .INFO are still most popular and preferable domain names to use.

## Using a hosting service

Web hosting is one of the crucial steps of web site building. Often this may be confusing and hard to decide about choosing a good and reliable hosting company.

**What is web hosting?**

It is a service that provides space for users to store their website content. Website information such as images, videos, or any other content accessible through the web needs to be stored on a computer server located in a secure and climate controlled environment which is permanently connected to the Internet through high speed data lines. This server space is called as web hosting.

There are numerous and various web hosting companies, services on the Internet. They differ from each other by their prices, services and qualities.

Often finding an optimal and appropriate hosting service may be an overwhelming process, especially for new web site creators.

Here are some guides for choosing a good hosting service:

- **Don't chase free web hostings.** Although free service sounds good, later it may not be so effective as it has seemed before. If you wish to earn money by using your web site, you have to find reliable and assured services which can take responsibilities by their side.

- **Choose a host, not a price.** Price is not a sign of web host quality. Take a little bit time and make a research about what kind of services they offer.

- **Try short term contracts before.** Like most other services web hosting also offers some discounts for long term contracts and asks for advance payments for multi month or yearly contracts. I strongly recommend to try out a new hosting service for one or two months and also ensure the contract termination and money back policies before.

- **Separately register your domain name.** If something goes wrong with your web host, there will not be a chance to detain your domain name too.

- **Efficient customer support.** Usually admirable customer services may save your time and prevent some future frustrations. Connect with a customer support team for solving any issue that you have and check its quality and efficiency before making any decisions. It should be easy to get in touch with and they should help you in a nice and professional way.

- *Find a hosting service that proclaims down times.* Usually web hosts frequently update their servers and in this case your site will also be unavailable when this process happens. Therefore, select  a service that tells you in advance when your site will be down. Updating procedure should be when you are not getting lots of visits.

- *Pick a company that offers you detailed site statistics.* It is better choose a hosting service that suggests statistics and traffic info to your website.

- *Choose secure payment methods.* Make sure that hosting service accepts well-known and secure payment methods.

## Establishing a website

As statistics shows most people don't read online while surfing on web pages, they just scan. They stop scanning whenever something catches their attention. When something captures their interest, then they will read it deeper and in details. This is very considerable factor in website building and designing. If you create and design your web site properly and professionally this will bring you a high amount of traffic.

But designing a website or webpage demands some knowledge, skills, tricks and abilities. Especially, this may be hard for beginners and I recommend these people to recruit a web designer if they are not able to do it for themselves.

While establishing your website or webpage you should seriously pay attention to web page layout.

Website layout is a setting of different elements that creates a website. This includes creating a web page structure; choosing a theme, color, fonts, graphics and logo; inserting multimedia files; setting menu and navigation buttons; linking ads, mailing, etc.

Search on the Internet for "website layout tips and tricks", find and make a little research about them. Dedicate your two or three hours for studying website layout building and designing techniques.

## Writing a content

Creating a well organized, concise and attractive content is a vital part of web building. It is not as easy as it seems and for this reason most website owners recruit professional content writers.

There are 2 types of content: *Story type* and *Editorial type*.

### Story type of content

In this type of content you can write a short story about how you (or someone) achieved something by using the product or service you are promoting. Here you should illustrate to your audience how the person you are telling about was similar to them and then got positive results by using the product or service you are inviting them too. Usually people search for solution to their problems and maybe that's why they have found you.

### Editorial type of content

In this type you have to write a professional article relevant to the product you are promoting.

Here are some tips that may help you for writing a successful content:

- *Use bulleted lists to express your ideas.* When you are writing about something you may list its advantages and disadvantages, its specifics, its benefits and others by using bulleted lists. This method helps your website visitors to understand you better, easier and faster.

- *Use bold, italic, underlined and uppercase writing techniques.* If you want your keywords or terms to be seen easily, just use these above mentioned techniques to emphasize them. Without any doubt, highlighted words or sentences will be displayed initially to the eyes of viewer than the ones that were not distinguished.

- *Don't create long paragraphs.* As statistics shows people usually tend to read short sections than long ones. If they are prolonged and tedious, they will jump from long paragraphs to shorter ones or even leave this webpage.

- **Create a catchy title.** Well selected name or title is a half success in any business. The chosen title should reveal what the issue is about and totally the main meaning of the subject you are writing.

- **Be objective.** Avoid from flashing and boasting *"This is the best..."* claims and instead let people come to that conclusion on their own.

- **Use a reversed pyramid method of writing.** Write your main ideas, points and conclusion on the first page of the text. Most web readers are impatient and don't want to read the topic until the end.

- **Use right keywords.** Appropriate keywords in content writing are special words which people use while searching on the Internet. Apply at least 100-300 important keywords in your content and arrange them at the beginning and also at the end of your content. Make sure that you have not overused keywords, but you have spread them over your content wisely and normally.

- ***Write an original content.*** Plagiarism will be punished by search engines. So, make a little research and create your own content.

- ***Insert pictures or videos.*** Adding eye-catching and cute images which are related to your content will capture visitors' attention and makes them glance for a moment.

- ***Check spelling and grammar.*** Spelling and grammar mistakes make people stop reading and jump to another websites. Proofread your content before embedding them into your web pages.

## SEO (Search Engine Optimization)

Search engine optimization is an aggregate of various optimizing strategies and techniques used to boost the ranking of a website in search engine results page like Google, Yahoo, Bing, etc.

Usually website owners try to improve their website's ranking in search results by optimizing its content and structure. They want it to be recognized by search engines.

Usually SEO reveals the secrets of how search engines work, what people search for and which keywords they use and many others.

If you have a website and want it to be seen on the top page of search results, you will need to know about the nuances of SEO. Surely, without knowing and using SEO techniques all your other efforts on website building will be worthless. If so, don't be unconcerned about Search Engine Optimization.

There are hundreds of SEO tips, tricks and strategies which are available to use for affiliates. But I appreciated to list only these crucial ones:

- **Write a unique content.** Don't copy others' content. Search engines punish your website if you have copied someone else's content.

- **Use proper keywords**. Utilize appropriate keywords and phrases in your content, text body, titles, headlines, domain, URLs, etc. But, pay attention to keywords' density and don't repeat them too much.

- *Make links.* Try to get relevant links from other top ranked and famous websites and social media. Make sure that these links also go to other pages of your site.

- *Apply sitemaps.* Site map is a tool for growing easy navigation across the website. This helps web users promptly and efficiently search every page of the website.

- *Optimize website.* Usually long time loading of a web page makes site visitors disappointed and not wait until it's opening. It is better not increase 100k page size and decrease unnecessary characters from web pages.

- *Set up social network.* Create and share your posts and articles in social media like Facebook, Twitter, YouTube, etc. Ensure inserting your domain name and other relevant links there.

Don't forget! The higher your website rank in search results, the more visitors and traffic it will receive.

**Recommended websites:**

## Domain registrars:

- www.godaddy.com

- www.webweaverelite.com

- www.namecheap.com

- www.register.com

- www.networksolutions.com

## Web hosting:

- www.hostgater.com

- www.bluehost.com

- www.web.com

- www.justhost.com

- www.ipage.com

## Theme creating:

- www.wordpress.com

- www.elegantthemes.com

- www.woothemes.com

- www.studipress.com

- www.themeforestcom

## Mailing providers:

- www.aweber.com

- www.getresponse.com

- www.icontact.com

Campaign tracking:

- www.prosper202.com

- www.alexa.com

Choosing right keywords:

- www.googlekeywordtool.com

- www.adwods.google.com

- www.seoquake.com

- www.keywordelite.com

Website tools creator:

- www.veripurchase.com

- www.mcafee.com

- www.hirewriters.com

- www.easywebinarplugin.com

- www.webceo.com

Search Engine Optimization (SEO):

- www.searchenginesubmitter.com

# Blogs

## What is a blog?

Blog is a form of website that is generally arranged in chronological order from the most recent posts to the older ones towards the bottom just like a diary or journal.

It is a personal online publishing method which lets individuals simply and quickly write, publish and distribute almost everything on any matter via Internet.

As web sites blogs also include text entries, graphics, videos, comments, links with other websites, etc.

Often most affiliate marketers use blogs within their web sites and also separately from it. There are thousands of affiliates who are using web blogs as their promotional, communicative and informative target.

**There are some big and crucial advantages of using blogs for affiliate marketers:**

- Starting a blog is easier and quicker than starting a website;
- Mostly it doesn't cost anything to start;

- Huge opportunity of reaching hundreds or thousands of people in a day;
- An effective way of promoting affiliate products or services;
- A chance for building credibility and positioning yourself as an expert in the field you have chosen, etc.

It is clear that blog creating doesn't require lots of knowledge and skills like website building. Therefore today on the Internet exist more than 100 million blogs which most of them are created by ordinary people like you and me.

There are some very popular and trusted blogger web sites like www.blogger.com and www.wordpress.com which may be very easy and quick to launch even for newbie affiliate marketers. But before starting to blog I have decide to provide you with some useful tips and tricks for preventing some future troubles that may occur on your way.

**Here are some helpful tips for creating a successful blog:**

- *Identify your intention.* For preventing future troubles define your long term plans before choosing free or paid blogging.
- *Target your audience.* Create a blog for them with a content that they are looking for.
- *Write a good content*. Creating a high quality content is a vital part of blogging. Recruit your all best possibilities and techniques for writing a genius and exciting content.
- *Build credibility.* Appear as a trusted and expert person in the eyes of your visitors. Usually people estimate you by the result of the assist you have given to them. Always remember the golden principle of a successful affiliate marketer: *"First help, then offer"*.
- *Don't be "a promotion person".* Putting *"subscribe"* or *"click here to buy"* links or buttons all over the pages makes your visitors displeased and annoyed. Try to be modest and helpful until people trust you and like your blog more.
- *Make your blog simple.* Create an attractive, easy to navigate and simple blog.

- *Use a clean and simple theme.* Don't apply heavy and tiresome themes.

- *Recruit a freelancer.* If you have a possibility, use a freelance service for developing your blog.

- *Post regularly*. This is a simple and effective way for adding more traffic to your website or blog. As an active blogger write helpful posts daily and consistently. Try to create at least one blog post everyday for getting good results and also avoid from writing long and complex ones.

**Recommended websites:**

- www.blogger.com
- www.wordpress.com

# Online discussion communities

Online discussion community is a virtual community where people interact with each other by posting their opinions, messages, information, etc.

As online discussion communities there may be chat rooms, discussion boards, blogs, forums, social networks, etc.

Attending in online communities may be a great and productive way for being acknowledged as an expert in your chosen affiliate field.

Below I have listed several key points of using a forum as a promoting method in affiliate marketing:

- **Join with top ranked forums.** Make sure that there is high traffic pending to the forum you are attending in. Choose and register on the forums where high amount of people are concerned.

- **Discussion boards should be related to the product you are promoting.** Just search using keywords such as *"forum"* or *"discussion board"* with the subject of the affiliates you are promoting. For example, if you are promoting skin care products, search for *"skin care products forum"*.

- **Participate actively**. This may help you to boost your affiliate income when members see you as an active and trusted person. Provide requests with the answers that are really helpful and problem solving for people. If people find you as a person who solves their issues they will also be eager to click the link you have provided in your signature box or just attempt to connect with you. Try to be an authority in the subject you discuss.

- **Review member policies**. Because some online communities may prohibit affiliate links and consider the links as advertising spam.

- **Don't directly insert affiliate links in your posts.** Forum members dislike these people who usually just write something with flashing affiliates links. Don't be this person. At the end of your post there is a signature box where you can put a promotional text and also affiliate links. This signature box will be displayed each time you reply to or write your posts.

**Recommended websites:**

- www.big-boards.com
- www.forums.digitalpoint.com

- www.warriorforum.com

# Viral products

Viral product is a digital product that is intended to spread very quickly to a large number of people. This can be a short twenty or thirty pages book, a 200 or 300 words containing article or special report, an amateur made video, etc.

Using viral products in affiliate marketing is a great and free method without ever having a website.

Usually applying viral products in affiliate marketing means creating it on a particular subject, inserting affiliate links into there and distributing it through whatever you like. You may distribute your viral products to people for giving it away or selling. Also you may submit them on hundreds of article directories and get them published on most websites over the Internet.

**Article writing**

Writing articles or promoting affiliate stuffs by using this free method is not as hard as it seems to most people.

Today on the Internet thousands of online marketers are utilizing articles as their fast and easy success getting technique. Because it is one of the most helpful ways of advertising and selling affiliate stuffs.

Here are some major steps and tips about it:

- **Write only high value articles.** As bestseller books online articles also should be high quality, helpful, problem solving, interesting, etc. If you aim your article to be sold in a high amount, learn before how to find solutions for readers' problems and issues which are afflicting them.
- **Use keywords properly.** You should apply exact keywords about the subject and distribute them throughout the article with an average density. But if you overuse keywords, search engines will mark your article as a spam and make it not appear in search engine results.
- **Optimal length.** The length of the article should be 350-1,400 words. Don't write a long reading and boring articles.

- *Choose a catchy title.* When a person views the heading of a written article he or she will be too skeptical to read it entirely. Therefore, choose an attractive and attention grabbing title for your articles.

- *Use article directory websites.* Article directory web sites are those that contain a list of articles of different topics. They allow you to register for an account, submit your article and publish it in their web site for free.

- *Review the policies of each website you join.* Some article directory websites may limit the amount of affiliate links you can place into each article.

- *Bring more traffic.* Use keyword determiner tools wisely and make your article "Search Engine Optimized" for appearing it on the top page of search results.

## Book writing

If you are able to write books, this may be a great way for you to promote your affiliate products even without having your own website or web blog.

Just write an book related to the subject you are promoting, insert affiliates links and submit them in everywhere you want to be published and sold. If the readers like your book, then they may visit merchant's website and make a purchase. This is much more like article writing process, but unlike article writing you can also publish, sell your books separately and make a good profit from it.

So, you have a good written book and what now?

Publishing and distributing an book will not demand a great power and knowledge. If the book is written professionally, honestly and really helps people to solve their problems, believe me you will definitely get huge successes by publishing, distributing and selling it.

If your book is related to the affiliate issue and ready for being distributed online use below recommended book directories for publishing and handing out. There are hundreds of book directories on the Internet which range by their service qualities and prices. Some of them are paid services and others may be absolutely for free. Rules and the process of publishing books are explained in every directory and you may be familiar with them by entering these websites and reviewing their policies.

**Recommended websites:**

Article writing:

- www.goarticles.com

- www.articlemarketer.com

- www.ezinearticles.com

- www.articlesbase.com

- www.articlecity.com

- www.isnare.com

- www.topezineads.com

- www.directoryofezines.com

Book writing:

- www.book-marketing-revealed.com

- www.ebookdirectory.com

- www.wisdomebooks.com

- www.elibrary.com

# Social media marketing

## What is social media marketing?

Today it's clear for every Internet user that social media networks widely opened the doors of various, comfortable and easy opportunities of communication via online.

Nowadays even people who rarely use Internet are familiar with the power and opportunities of social networks like Facebook, Twitter Google+, YouTube, Pinterest, etc.

In our days people are not only using social media as a popular method of communication, but also utilizing it as a powerful and indispensable marketing tool which brings various positive results almost in every business.

## So, what is social media marketing?

Social media marketing is one of the types of internet marketing which serves to realize various marketing communications through social media networks.

By interacting and sharing different contents, information, news, links, resources via social networks individuals or companies may establish easy relationship between each other and reach their some valuable business goals.

**Benefits of social media marketing in affiliate business**

Today it is well known for almost every affiliate marketer that applying social media networks as a communicating and marketing tool is vitally important, irreplaceable and winning strategy for running successful affiliate businesses.

It has many and particular advantages for affiliates to market their business. Here are some of them:

- Social media gives you a chance to generate more links to your website;
- Using it properly brings massive traffic to your website and boosts your SEO;
- Social media facilitates you to get a larger audience;
- It costs you almost nothing to establish this word of mouth advertising in social networks, etc.

**Social media tips for affiliate marketing**

- **Don't just promote**. Social media is created for communication, not for advertising something online. Imagine if you like or follow people in social networks and they only send you advertising links, will you then stop following them? Will it be unpleasant for you to get such promoting links? Of course "Yes". Try to set up a valuable interaction between you and others. As attending in online forums being a "valuable person" in social media is also very important.

- **Use all possible social media platforms.** Don't just use most famous social media like Facebook, Twitter or Google+. If you have created a website make sure that you have established several different social media networks.

- **Interact productively.** Try to communicate with your customers regularly. Make discussions about the topics related to the products or services you are presenting.

- **Optimize your social media.** Social media optimization means making a website visible and noticeable to the viewers in social media sites.

**Recommended websites:**

Social media networking:

- www.facebook.com
- www.twitter.com
- www.linkedin.com
- www.pinterest.com

# Revenue sharing websites

Revenue sharing websites are free website platforms which allow users to create free web pages on the subjects that they are passionate about or interested in. The biggest uniqueness of these platforms is that they don't demand from users being aware of website creating and designing skills. They allow users to build pages on various topics, insert ads, reviews, content and others without having to write any HTML.

Commonly the purpose of creating such free web pages may be different. Some of the users establish pages there just for passion, others for promoting or selling their or others' products.

Today websites as Squidoo, Hubpages, Bukisa, InfoBarrel, Xomba, Ukritic and others have been already popular on the Internet. Especially most affiliates who don't have their own web pages or blogs will be eager to use them as an additional promoting method.

In some cases affiliates can use these revenue sharing web sites effectively. They can turn them into link building, traffic generating and referral tools.

Every revenue sharing website has its own pros and cons. The strategy that recommended for one affiliate marketer may not work for another one. I recommend you to learn and try them personally. Below I've provided you with the list of some necessary and useful revenue sharing websites.

**Recommended websites:**

Revenue sharing:

- www.squidoo.com
- www.hubpages.com
- www.bukisa.com
- www.infobarrel.com

- www.xomba.com
- www.ukritic.com

# Conclusion

Gradually finishing my book I've decided to write about some very important tips and key points of affiliate marketing success. If you want to be a successful affiliate marketer, don't be inattentive to these tips.

**Helpfulness**

Almost in every case people hesitate about the value of the products or services which they are going to purchase. If the output seems worthless they will surely decide not to deal with it.

Why they should pay for something which doesn't bring them any favor?

So, make sure that your being proposed products or services are really problem solving and helpful.

Replace yourself with a potential customer and ask this question from yourself *"Would you buy it if you were in the place of the customer?"* If the answer is *"Yes"*, then the product you are promoting is really helpful and high quality. If the answer is *"No"*, then the product you are promoting is surely not helpful and low quality.

## Honesty

Affiliate marketing is all about trust. If you want to be successful in this business promote only products that you also believe in. Just help people with your products or services and think only about how to solve their problems. Removing severity from their shoulders and making them happy brings you real value and more capital.

## Patience

Affiliate marketing is not a get rich quick business. Succeeding in this field and seeing good results may take a little time. Don't give up if you don't see instant profits.

## Activism

Be always active and don't wait people someday come to you. You have to be proactive by using techniques like link building, SEO and social media marketing if you want to get your site noticed and get people click on your affiliate links.

## Focusing

Don't immediately choose promoting many different products on the particular site. Most successful affiliates recommend promoting each unique product on a different website.

Make sure that you have focused on and provided your customers with enough information about the product you are promoting.

## Knowledge

Always be eager to getting new comprehensions about affiliate marketing. Seek for new success tips, strategies, tricks, etc. Being successful demands well planned actions and smart decisions. Also learn how other affiliates have been successful in their business and what kind of mistakes they have done.

## Freebies

Good marketers always use the marvelous possibilities of various discounts, freebies and gifts. Without any doubt these marketing strategies invoke good impressions in the mind of people. Don't tire of proposing free offers to the people who are interested in your products or services.

## Relationship

Keep always good relationships with the people you are dealing with. This may be your website members, customers, other friendly affiliates or just any people who are interested in your activity.

## Tracking

Tracking your campaigns makes your work easier and helps you to control your activities. For example, in ClickBank you can write a name or a memo note on the *"ID field"*. Though it's an optional, I appreciate it as a key factor. Because this technique helps you to know about the process: who is buying your which product. Analyzing your individual campaigns is critical for determining whether you're on the right path or you need to make any changes in your strategy.

And always remember! Whatever you do any business online or offline be helpful and frank to the people. When you give them what they really need, believe me sooner or later you will get a huge value instead. If you want to see this with your own eyes, just start to act now!

**Good luck!**

www.ingramcontent.com/pod-product-compliance
Lightning Source LLC
Chambersburg PA
CBHW071812170526
45167CB00003B/1278